My Children Tried To Unwrap The Prophetic Gift God Gave Them

Carol Brown

Copyright © 2019 by Carol Brown

All rights reserved. No part of this publication may be reproduced by any means, graphics, electronic, or mechanical, including photocopying, recording, taping, or by any information storage retrieval system without the written permission of the publisher except in the case of brief quotations embodied in critical articles and reviews.

Carol Brown/Rejoice Essential Publishing
PO BOX 512
Effingham, SC 29541

www.republishing.org

Unless otherwise indicated, scripture is taken from the King James Version.

Scripture quotations marked (NIV) are taken from the Holy Bible, New International Version®, NIV®. Copyright © 1973, 1978, 1984, 2011 by Biblica, Inc.™ Used by permission of Zondervan. All rights reserved worldwide. www.zondervan.com The "NIV" and "New International Version" are trademarks registered in the United States Patent and Trademark Office by Biblica, Inc.™

Scripture taken from the New King James Version®. Copyright © 1982 by Thomas Nelson. Used by permission. All rights reserved.

Scripture quotations marked (ESV) are taken from The Holy Bible, English Standard Version® (ESV®) Copyright © 2001 by Crossway, a publishing ministry of Good News Publishers.

All rights reserved.

Scripture quotations marked (NLT) are taken from the Holy Bible, New Living Translation, copyright ©1996, 2004, 2015 by Tyndale House Foundation. Used by permission of Tyndale House Publishers, Carol Stream, Illinois 60188. All rights reserved.

My Children Tried To Unwrap The Prophetic Gift God Gave Them/ Carol Brown

ISBN-13: 978-1-952312-68-7

Library of Congress Control Number: 2021907126

Dedication

To my family, people in our community always remind me of how I adore "my" husband Victor, my four children: Rory Jr., Terrica, Victor II, Adrian, Nichols. I want to thank you all for being there for me. I would not have ever gotten through this without God and my Family.

To my wonderful husband Victor, I think the world of you. Thank you for being there for me and allowing me the time to spend with the Lord, so I could hear from God to write this book.

To my eldest daughter, Terrica, thank you for praying and encouraging me to be strong.

I want to thank a few special people. Thank you, Apostle Tim and Carolyn Kurtz, my spiritual father and mother. Thank you, Sister Kathryn Wheeler, for helping me start writing this book. Thank you, Sister Tammy Lee, for all of your prayers. May God continue to bless them.

Table of Contents

INTRODUCTION:	God Is A Gift Giving God; He Gives The Gift Of Salvation	1
CHAPTER 1:	You Can't Deny the Call	6
CHAPTER 2:	The Only Way You Can Unwrap the Gift	9
CHAPTER 3:	Receiving the Gifts of the Spirit	14
CHAPTER 4:	Turning My Life Back To You	19
CHAPTER: 5:	Prepare For Action	23
CHAPTER 6:	We Must Surrender	27
CHAPTER 7	Take Your Position and Stand	34

CHAPTER 8	Unwrapping God's Perfect Gift......39
CHAPTER 9	Activating the prophetic gifts......47
CHAPTER 10	What is Saving Grace?......57

ABOUT THE AUTHOR......61

Introduction

GOD IS A GIFT GIVING GOD; HE GIVES THE GIFT OF SALVATION

To be saved is to live. The Bible declares in John 3:16-17 (NKJV), "For God so loved the world that He gave His only begotten Son, that whoever believes in Him should not perish but have everlasting life. For God did not send His Son into the world to condemn the world, but that the world through Him might be saved."

Salvation is also a gift of God's grace and cannot be obtained through works. It is freely given to those who put their faith in the finished work of Jesus Christ on the cross and confess Jesus as Lord.

To be saved means that we have eternal life, which means spending eternity with God, who dwells in us. The true meaning of life is being reconciled to God for all eternity.

The Bible tells us that Christians should be committed to reconciling people to God. In 2 Corinthians 5:18-20, Paul tells us that God has given us the ministry of reconciliation with others and God. Our response to God's saving grace is expressed through our response to others.

HOW DO I BECOME SAVED?

Romans 10:9 says, "That if you confess with your mouth the Lord Jesus and believe in your heart that God has raised Him from the dead, you will be saved."

Now after receiving God into our lives, we must now walk in our gift of salvation. My children struggled initially with this concept because they did not fit in with their friends. When problems came up against them, they remembered quickly who God is and the precious gift of salvation.

They would come home from a party and say, "Mom and dad, we really should listen to you. We truly experienced the devil at work. We saw some parents hanging with their kids and getting high with them. We are glad you guys are saved and you don't hang with us in the night clubs. We truly realize we do need salvation."

Salvation as being a gift, which it is. Romans 6:23 says, "For the wages of sin is death, but the gift of God is eternal life in Christ Jesus our Lord." Salvation is a gift because it is something that is not earned. Romans 4:4 (ESV) says, "Now to the one who works, his wages are not counted as a gift but as his due."

Some may feel like the gift of salvation is unnecessary or refuse to accept it. They may even feel this gift is not valuable like a Styrofoam cup or a ceramic goose cookie jar. Nothing could be further from the truth.

One of the primary reasons people reject Christ as their Savior is being blind to their need for saving. Either they don't believe there is a God to be accountable to, or they consider themselves good enough to merit salvation on their own. So the gospel does not compel them. They find it easy to disregard the message of the cross as a peculiar exercise in humility for those inclined to subjugate themselves. Also they feel it is a fanciful, guilt inclined tale propagated by religious institutions bent on subjugating others. There is an interesting exchange between Jesus and the Pharisees recorded in Chapter 9 of John's Gospel. Jesus had just performed a miraculous healing where a man born blind could see. The Pharisees had their self-righteous knickers in a twist because Jesus healed on the Sabbath. In responding of faith...

Jesus said, "For Judgment I come into this world that those who do not see may see, and those who see may become blind. " Some of the Pharisees near him heard these things, and said to him, Are we also blind?" Jesus said to them, "If you were blind, you would have no guilt: but now that you say, 'We see,' your guilt remains,"- John 9:39-41 (ESV)

CHAPTER 1

You Can't Deny the Call

Jeremiah 1:5 (NIV)
"Before I formed you in the womb I knew you, before you were born I set you apart; I appointed you as a prophet to the nations."

Well, I have four children. They were all called by God to some form of ministry. I, as their mother, have trained them up in the Lord. The Bible says to "Train up a child in the way he should go and when he or she grows old, they will not depart from it" (Proverbs 22:6).

My mother sent me to worship service. My grandparents, Fred and Clara McGee took me to Sunday service. *The Young People Willing Workers* (YPWW) youth department brought me to church to attend the "Watch Night" prayer meeting. Here is when I started learning the Bible and to pray at watch night. I would watch the older women and men pray. I believe this prayer style passed down to me and then down to my children then my grandchildren. It went from generation to generation as a generational blessing. As a result, breaking all generational cruises. Genesis 12:3 (ESV) says, "I will bless those who bless you, and him who dishonors you I will curse, and in you all the families of the earth shall be blessed."

Yes, I learned about God at an early age. I don't know why my children thought they could get away from being a part of the Kingdom of God. This same God was passed down to me and now I am passing Him down to them. And they will pass Him down to their children. There is such a thing as generational curses as well as generational blessings. We were blessed to have a blood line of generational blessings. Although there were generational curses that tried to overtake our whole family, God said not so. I always remind my children that God set you apart from darkness before you were born and formed you into light, for the plans He has for you, so don't deny the call He has on your life. You can run, but you can not hide, so just stay in place and get ready for what He called you to do.

Every time they tried to get out of place with the Lord, He would deal with them. It was a point where all four of my children tried to run at the same time. They were placed in an organization or facility. Three were in shelters and one was in a drug-free facility. God brought them down to nothing, then rebuild them back up into the mind of Him. He said, "Not your will, but My will be done in you. I want to make you followers of Me and not of man. It's time to come from among those unclean things and live life for Me." It did not happen overnight. It was a timely transformation. One child has the anointing of David. The other has an Esther anointing. Another has the Deborah anointing. One has the Jacob anointing.

CHAPTER 2

The Only Way You Can Unwrap the Gift

I told my children that the only way to unwrap the "gift" is that they must understand who they are in Christ. They must search for the "gift" that God gave them.

Through the struggles and stresses of this world that tries to overtake them, they still press to serve God. I told my children to stand up and protect themselves, for God is here to help us. Every time they tried to find their rest in drugs, girls, men, money, etc., they would always have to turn back to God and the "Gift" He gave them. They found the only way to unwrap the "gift" was through salvation and seeking God for it. There is a song by Commission titled, "Running Back To You." Some lyrics are "I keep running back to You and Your arms are open wide." Their minds were on the nightclub, but at that moment, God spiritually arrested them and they found Him. It was the relationship with God that was so important, not the people, or the things.

I remember past Christmases. My brothers, sisters, and I could not wait to open our gifts so we could see who was going to get the most special present under the tree. Those gifts under that tree were so beautiful. They were wrapped in all types of beautiful paper with big bows.

The tree was decorated with colorful lights and ornaments.

Your gift carries value and you cannot go anywhere without knowing it. You must know how valuable your identity is. What is so amazing about this revelation is I wrote this book in the COVID-19 pandemic. My children and I were faced with tragedy by the great suffering, destruction, distress, and unhappiness. So many people lost their lives from an incurable virus. We battled with this virus for over a year and had to quarantine. It was a place of hibernation as well as consecration.

Matthew 13:44-46 (ESV) says, "The kingdom of heaven is like treasure hidden in a field, which a man found and covered up. Then in his joy he goes and sells all that he has and buys that field. Again, the kingdom of heaven is like a merchant in search of fine pearls, who, on finding one pearl of great value, went and sold all that he had and bought it."

I feel God moved us into a place of seeking Him at a greater level to know Him even more. I believe this is how we were able to find our true identity by opening up our Word and unwrapping the gifts to understand what was really going on. Doing this time, we thought we had it together, but really we didn't. In the midst of the storm, our hearts started dating our gifts to know if we had the true salvation of God.

When you received the gift of Salvation, you are wrapped with His robe of righteousness and covered under His wing (Psalms 91). When you unwrap these "gifts" you start to shine like those lights and then people begin to see the gift of God and the beauty of God in His Image. The deep treasure in life is not missing anything and needs to be found in the true image of God. When someone finds the treasures of God within us, they will find nothing but His true revelation, so they will be drawn to the Kingdom.

- Study to show thyself approved .... (2 Tim. 2:15)

It is His truth by the washing of God's Word that will make us free. We are to be that beautiful church called Zion or Ekklesia (Greek word), which is the assembly of the people or congregation that will bring forth His light and overtake the darkness in our life. Light will bring change. It will unwrap those gifts He gave to all man. When we dig deep in God, we will find the treasure He wants to unfold in our lives. Let us seek for Him and we will receive Him.

CHAPTER 3

Receiving the Gifts of the Spirit

I believe that every child of God is a candidate to receive a gift of the Holy Spirit. It is important to understand what the gifts of the Spirit are and that we do not neglect using what the Holy Spirit imparts to us.

Ignorance comes through a lack of knowledge. If we don't know about these gifts, how will we be able to desire and experience them? 1 Corinthians 12:1 says, "Now concerning spiritual gifts brethren I would not have you ignorant." Romans 12:6 says, "Having those gifts differing according to the grace that is given to you." 1 Timothy 4:14 says, "Neglect not the gift that is in thee." We should never let this gift lay dormant and unused in our lives.

Every child of God who has been baptized with His Spirit may know and experience the nine gifts of the Holy Spirit.

Many times, my family and I have operated in the gifts of the Spirit. For example, to have a strong marriage, we must have the Word of Knowledge and the Word of Wisdom. When my husband and I first got married, we had a hard time working together in just about anything. We had some miscommunication about finances and other areas. It seemed like Satan had us going until we received the Knowledge of God. Then we were able to hear by God's Spirit and not by our flesh. As a result, when frustration tried to come in, we learned to seek God in pray, fasting, the Logos (the written Word of God), and the Rhema Word (the spoken Word of God). My husband and I have been married for 30 years. People always asked how did we do it? It's only by God's grace and following His principles. We could not have done it any other way. Even raising our children, we had to operate out of the gifts of the Spirit to overcome challenges. You try coming out of a family with a background of dysfunctionality. We have a blended family. One child thought we loved the other children more. If you want God to work in your family, then it will take having the gifts of the Spirit operating in your lives.

Allow God's plans for your life to be fulfilled. An example of the Word of Knowledge is found in John 4:1-26. Jesus talked to the Samaritan woman. The Holy Spirit revealed to Him information about her married life (verse 18). You can see how useful the Word of Knowledge would be in counseling someone. Another example of the Word of Knowledge is found in Matthew

12:1-9. Jesus told his disciples to get a donkey to ride into Jerusalem. He knew exactly where the donkey was located. How did He know the donkey was there? The Word of Knowledge is also called a message of Knowledge. It is a Gift of the Supernatural information that is not available to you naturally.

The nine Gifts of the Holy Spirit or diversities of gifts given by the Holy Spirit (1 Corinthians 12: 8-11)

Remember, we can ask God for these Gifts to manifest in our lives.

The nine gifts mentioned in 1 Corinthian 12 are

1. the Word of Wisdom
2. the Word of Knowledge
3. Faith
4. Gifts of Healing
5. Working of Miracles
6. Prophecy
7. Discerning of the Spirits
8. Different kinds of Tongues

9. Interpretation of Tongues

THE THREE REVELATION GIFTS

A. Word of Wisdom
B. Knowledge
C. Discerning of the Spirits

THREE POWER GIFTS

A. Faith
B. Gifts of healing
C. Working of miracles

THREE VOCAL GIFTS

A. Prophecy
B. Divers kinds of tongues
C. Interpretation

CHAPTER 4

Turning My Life Back To You

I found that my life is lost without you Lord. I need you at first hand. Lord, I ask you to operate on me? Make me brand new. Give me the mind of Christ. God make me more like you. Philippians

2:5-6 says, " Let this mind be in you, which was also in Christ Jesus: Who, being in the form of God, thought it not robbery to be equal with God."

David said in Psalm 51:10-11, "Create in me a clean heart. O God, renew a right spirit in me. Cast me not away from thy presence; and take not thy Holy Spirit from me."

Transform my thoughts as I press forward to the high call in you oh, Lord. This means to exert, deliberate, or maximum effort for his purpose of reaching or attaining it. We must be like runners in a race or drivers for the finish line (Philippians 3:14). You told me that you would never leave me nor will you forsake me (Hebrews 13:5). Lord, the only way I can unwrap this gift that you gave me, I must follow your will. I can run, but I found every time I try to do things on my on it won't work. I just can't hide from you Lord. To be free, I must follow your plan. For you know the plans you have for me. Jeremiah 29:11says, "For I know the plans I have for you," declares the Lord, plans to prosper you and not to harm you, plans to give you hope and a future.

Lord, I find my joy and peace in you. It's time to do this race and stay in it. Many times, my children ran away from God feeling hopeless because they felt this faith walk was too hard. They did not realize it takes time to become fully grown and mature in God. It did not happen until they read the Scriptures for themselves. Their salvation did not grow over night. It is like when a baby is born. We don't expect the baby to act like an adult. We give the baby at least 18 years to begin displaying adult-like behavior. Even then, our expectations are quite low. Sometimes it takes more than 20 years for a baby to mature. My children found it was no need to run but just summit to God, resist the devil, and he will flee.

James 4:7-8 says, "Submit yourselves, then, to God. Resist the devil, and he will flee from you. Come near to God and he will come near you." We must learn to battle Satan and our flesh by trusting in the promise of God. The connection of these two thoughts is no accident, for successful resistance flows from successful submission. A life that is totally submitted to God in every area is ironclad, completely impenetrable to Satan's attacks because it is fortified with godliness. We cannot afford to be passive when Satan or our flesh attempts to draw us away from obedience to Christ. In spiritual terms, we must learn to battle Satan and our flesh by trusting in the promise of God. The Lord promises to give us more grace and show favor to the humble (see James 4:6). When we live by such promises, we properly wield "the sword of the Spirit, which is the Word of God (Ephesians 6:17).

CHAPTER 5

Prepare For Action

My children learned to fight, as we all did as a family. We learned to gird up in God's truth to unwrap the beautiful gifts that He gave us for our life. We had to prepare for the battlefield.

1 Peter 1: 13 -16 says, "Therefore gird up the loins of your mind, be sober, and rest your hope fully upon the grace that is to be brought to you at the revelation of Jesus Christ; as obedient children not conforming yourselves to the former lusts, as in your ignorance; but as He who called you is holy, you also be holy in all your conduct, because it is written, "Be holy, for I am holy."

In the Greek, "Gird up the loins of your mind" uses imagery from Oriental custom.

They'd gather up the bottoms of their robes into their belt to free up their legs so they could run. Peter is telling us to get rid of whatever is holding us back. That race applies to the Christian life as well.

The armor of God is a very significant piece that we must learn to stand firm in by covering ourselves with the whole armor of God: the helmet, salvation, the breastplate of righteousness, the sword of the spirit, the shield of faith, the belt of truth, and the preparation of peace. — Ephesians 6:11-14

There is a positional component to the breastplate of righteousness. It is that we are righteous in Jesus through His death, burial, and resurrection, which is salvation by grace through faith.

You can't fight this battle alone. 2 Chronicles 20:15 says, "And he said Hearken ye, all Judah and ye inhabitants of Jerusalem, and thou King Jehoshaphat! Thus saith the Lord unto you: be not afraid nor dismayed by reason of the great multitude, for the Battle is Not Yours But God's."

God asked His children, "What's the battle that you're facing right now?"

Three thousand years ago, God's people faced their own battle. Victory came, but only after the struggle. And it came in the most unlikely of ways. The lesson they first had to learn was this:

This battle is not for you to fight; take your position, stand still, and see the victory of the Lord on your behalf.

This lesson was seen in the story of Jehoshaphat, found in 2 Chronicles 20:1-30.

Through the Scriptures and through building our relationship with God, we found to tear away from ourselves by moving into His true image.

We poured in His word, sought His face through prayer and fasting. God said, "Seek and you shall find. Knock and the doors will be opened."

God told us just show up and receive the gifts, treasures, and goods that He had for us. His main desire is that we would fall in love with Him and become intimate.

There are gifts with wrapping paper that God will unfold. Life and beauty will be revealed. We found God is the true answer to everything that we need. Nothing should be able to separate us from the love of God.

CHAPTER 6

We Must Surrender

We must render our lives and submit to God. We are no longer living according to this world. We don't walk with our own strength, but we live it by grace and faith. Talking about transformation, we are no longer living to a religious system. We have to surrender totally to God. Your gift carries value. You cannot go anywhere without knowing your gift. God is about to reboot your gift so you can carry value. Your gifts have to be cultivated. It has to be unwrapped with gentleness. You just can't rip the gift when you submit to God. You must handle your gifts with care. Surrendering to God is showing complete faith in Him and believing in His promises. Just like a child, we can walk in freedom from worry. We simply must choose to trust God for everything. If we can trust God for our Salvation through Jesus Christ, we can trust Him for our daily needs and desires.

Truly I tell you unless you change and become like little children you will never enter the kingdom of heaven.—Matthew 18:3 (NIV)

WHAT TO SURRENDER

Everything! Surrendering is literally giving up all control. It is telling God that we are not enough to deal with our worries and He must take over when we finally let go of all of our fears. We give God to will His mighty arm in our lives when our hands are weak and tired. God's hands are strong and powerful.

Powerful is your arm. Strong is your hand. Your right hand is lifted high in glorious strength. — Psalms 89:13 (NLT)

HOW TO SURRENDER

Surrendering control is a choice that we must make daily. Like every disciple in life, we must learn to surrender and give it to God. The enemy seeks every day to cloud our minds with worry, doubts, and fears. The devil wants there to be no room left for God in our lives. Surrendering to God becomes a daily lifestyle giving it all to Him.

Whenever negative thoughts seek to invade our space, we must cut them off and command them to die immediately. God's mercies are new every morning, so what happened yesterday last year or a decade ago is completely gone. Carrying the pain around will take up space for God's goodness, grace, and favor. Renewing our mind in Christ means letting go of all the burdens He died to take from us.

The steadfast love of the Lord never ceases. His mercies never come to an end. They are new every morning. Great is your faithfulness. — Lamentations 3:22-23 (ESV)

LETTING GO OF CONTROL

Control is the hardest thing to give up because without it, we feel vulnerable, but we do not need to worry. God is already in control. We need to recognize His authority, move over, and let Him lead. He is the Creator of the universe, so we can trust Him with each day. Letting go is scary at first, but the freedom in our minds and hearts will be worth it.

And we know that for those who love God all things work together for good for those who are called according to His purposes.— Romans 8:28 (ESV)

LET GO OF WORRY

Worrying adds not a single day to our lives. Worrying oppresses us every second. Worry can literally affect not only our minds and hearts but our bodies. To worry does absolutely nothing positive. Surrender worry to God and watch your life float in His favor. My children learned to surrender to God.

Don't worry about anything. Instead pray about everything. Tell God what you need and thank Him for all He has done. - Philippians 4:6 (NLT)

LETTING GO OF MONEY

We tend to hold tightly to our money. Money can be coming. I don't know if we place it ahead of God. He wants to bless us, so we need to put our finances properly in His hands. God will take care of us. We simply need to surrender our money and obey His leading.

Keep your life free from love of money and be content with what you have for He has said, "I will never leave you nor forsake you." —Hebrews 13:5 (ESV)

LETTING GO OF YOUR RELATIONSHIP

Surrendering to God's sovereign will in our relationships shows that we trust Him with the people we care about. We can't be everyone's Savior and hero, but Jesus can. He died because He loves us all, including the people most precious to us. We can do everything in our power to love and care for others and trust God with the rest.

And if God cares so wonderfully for wildflowers that are here today and thrown into the fire tomorrow, he will certainly care for you. Why do you have so little faith?— Matthew 6:30 (NLT)

LETTING GO OF YOUR FUTURE

We can only change one day at a time. Living in the future robs us from the joy today. Each day is a gift and we miss it when we allow our minds to dwell on the unknown. We can trust God with our future so we can focus on today. Trying to control the future is like trying to control the wind. Contentment in today will prevent our eyes from wandering off tomorrow.

Therefore do not worry about tomorrow, for tomorrow will worry about itself. Each day has enough trouble of its own.— Matthew 6:34 (NIV)

CHAPTER 7

Take Your Position and Stand

My children didn't want to take their stand at one point in time. The enemy was always trying to defeat them, but God said, "Not so. You are my children. Nobody can take that away. Take your position and follow me. I am your God. Now stand up. It's no longer you but I."

2 Chronicles 20:15-18 (ESV) says, "And he said listen all Judah and inhabitant of Jerusalem and king of Jehoshaphat thus, say the LORD to you, 'Do not be afraid and do not be dismayed at this great horde for the battle is not yours but God's. Tomorrow go down against them behold they will come up by ascent ziz. You will find them at the end of the valley, east of the Wilderness of Jeruel. You will not need to fight in this battle stand firm Hold Your Position and see the salvation of the Lord on your behalf O Judah and Jerusalem; Do not be afraid and do not be dismayed. Tomorrow go out against them and the Lord will be with you. Them Jehoshaphat bowed with his head his face to the ground and all Judah and the inhabitants of Jerusalem fell down before the Lord worshipping the Lord."

These great Scriptures accounts for a godly King, Jehoshaphat of Jerusalem, who pulled the nation out of pagan worship and led them into worshipping the One true God. Jehoshaphat and his people had just been victorious in battle against the Moabites but now an even more evil and powerful army is marching against them. King Jehoshaphat took the people into a time of powerful prayer and praise. The Spirit of the Lord comes upon your Jahaziel, son of Zachariah and he prophesied an encouraging word from the Lord. It happens just as God declared it would and the enemy was defeated! This story is very encouraging because it reminds us that we have an enemy who intends to bring a battle across our paths, just like he did with the Israelites. However, that's not our focus. God promises that we will overcome and breakthrough into everything He has for us if we are pursuing His will. We will face the enemy, but we will have total victory. The Scriptures above clearly share a directive, which is praising the mighty King.

I believe that God is prophetically speaking to us in this hour. "Hold the course beloved. Don't be afraid. I won't abandon you. I have planned a very great purpose. It will achieve. Stand firm and hold your position, for you will see my deliverance and salvation. I am at work. My purpose and great promises are being released over you and being achieved, so stand," said the Lord.

Let's further examine 2 Chronicles 20:15-18.

Do not fear (vs. 15)!

Fear paralyzes us and achieves nothing. Fear never changes circumstances for the better. Fear contaminates faith and causes us to doubt and question everything God has said. Fear is the opposite of faith. Resist it!

Do not be dismayed (vs. 15)!

God didn't say that He will keep us from facing battles. However, during battles, we are not to be discouraged, disheartened, distraught, demoralized, or distressed. He is our God and fights for us. He is awesome, strong, and powerful!

The battle isn't ours (vs. 15, 17)!

God says, "You do not need to fight in the battle and not to be afraid. Do not be dismayed, for I am with you." Throughout the Bible, we can visualize pictures of God fighting on behalf of His people and bringing them to victory. Our God fights for us, so take heart.

Position yourself (vs 17)!

Positioning yourself means don't run or hide when the battle comes but stand on the front lines next to your brothers and sisters shoulder-to-shoulder looking unto God. Plant your feet firmly and stand together in prayer, facing the enemy. God will overcome our enemy and win the battle on our behalf. My children learn to fight and stand to stay in position.

Face your enemy with absolute confidence (vs. 17)!
You will not need to fight in this battle. Stand firm, hold your position, and see the salvation of the Lord on your behalf. Oh Judah and Jerusalem, do not be afraid and be dismayed. Go out against them tomorrow and the Lord will be with you.

Remain in your position (vs. 17)!
How and where you position yourself is extremely important for the battle's outcome. If you leave the fight and your position, you won't see His victory. So stay in place, keep praying and watch what God does. God promised and declared 2 Chronicles 20:17 over us.

CHAPTER 8

Unwrapping God's Perfect Gift

Thanks be to God for His inexpressible gift —
2 Corinthians 9:15

The Bible tells us about who God is and His plan to redeem the lost world. He accomplished that plan through His only Son, Jesus Christ. Wrapped in the flesh, Jesus is the greatest gift there ever was sent directly from God. Take some time to reflect on who Jesus is and all we have in Him.

Sufficient: we have everything we will ever need through Christ!

2 Corinthians 9:8 (ESV) says, "And God is able to make all grace abound to you so that having all sufficiency in all things at all times you may abound in every good work."

Enrichment: God's plan is to bring increase. Thank Him for His multiplied blessings.

2 Corinthians 9:11 (ESV) says, "You will be enriched in every way to be generous and every way which through us will produce thanksgiving to God."

Light and Lift: unquenchable light and life are in Christ.

John 1:4-5 (ESV) says, "In Him was life and the life was the light of men the light shineth in darkness and the darkness has not overcome it."

Abundant Grace: we received everything through Christ including grace to enjoy it.

John 1:16 (ESV) says, "For from his fullness we have all received grace upon grace."

God in Flesh: Christ is not of this world but he became human to redeem us.

John 1:14 (ESV) says, "And the Word became flesh and dwelt among us, and we have seen his glory, glory as of the only Son from the Father, full of grace and truth."

Lamb of God: John 1:29 says, "Christ alone takes away the sin of the world."

Risen Savior: through Jesus' resurrection, we are born again to living hope.

1 Peter 1:3 (ESV) says, "Blessed be the God and father of our Lord Jesus Christ according to his great Mercy he has caused us to be born again to a Living Hope through the resurrection of Jesus Christ from the dead."

Our keeper: Jesus guards and keeps us on our way to heaven.

1 Peter 1:4-5 (ESV) says, "To an inheritance that is imperishable undefiled and unfading kept in heaven for you who by God's power are being guarded through faith for a Salvation ready to be revealed in the last time."

Prophetically promised: Christ Jesus is God's long-promised King.

Micah 5:2 (ESV) says, "But you, O Bethlehem Ephrathah, who are too little to be among the clans of Judah, from you shall come forth for me one who is to be ruler in Israel, whose coming forth is from of old, from ancient days."

Assurance of all we need: God will meet our every need.

Romans 8:32 (ESV) says, "He who did not spare his own Son but gave him up for us all, how will he not also with him graciously give us all things?"

Grief Bearer: On the cross, Jesus took our punishment.

Isaiah 53:5-6 (ESV) says, "But he was pierced for our transgressions; he was crushed for our iniquities; upon him was the chastisement that brought us peace, and with his wounds we are healed. All we like sheep have gone astray; we have turned—every one—to his own way; and the LORD has laid on him the iniquity of us all."

Guilt Bearer: On the cross, Jesus bore our sins and sorrow.

≈

Isaiah 53:4 (ESV) says, "Surely he has borne our griefs and carried our sorrows; yet we esteemed him stricken, smitten by God, and afflicted."

Heart of God's Redemptive Plan: God promised man at the beginning of time the following Scripture:

Genesis 3:15 (ESV) says, "I will put enmity between you and the woman, and between your offspring[a] and her offspring; he shall bruise your head, and you shall bruise his heel."

Conquering King: Jesus is God's triumphant ruler who will rule with perfect justice.

Isaiah 9:6-7 (ESV) says, "For to us a child is born, to us a son is given; and the government shall be upon his shoulder, and his name shall be called Wonderful Counselor, Mighty God, Everlasting Father, Prince of Peace. Of the increase of his government and of peace there will be no end, on the throne of David and over his kingdom, to establish it and to uphold it with justice and with righteousness from this time forth and forevermore. The zeal of the LORD of hosts will do this."

Coming King: all our hope is in Christ's return in glory.

Act 1:11 (ESV) says, "and said, "Men of Galilee, why do you stand looking into heaven? This Jesus, who was taken up from you into heaven, will come in the same way as you saw him go into heaven."

Righteousness Judge: when Christ returns, there will be a day of judgment.

Matthew 25:31 (ESV) says, "When the Son of Man comes in his glory, and all the angels with him, then he will sit on his glorious throne."

Wordy ruler: Jesus Christ is the only one in heaven and earth who is worthy to reign.

Revelations 5:12 (ESV) says, "Worthy is the Lamb who was slain, to receive power and wealth and wisdom and might and honor and glory and blessing!"

Our world is temporary and troubled. Christ is the eternal prince of peace. Let Him dominate your focus. Turn your eyes upon Jesus and look full in His wonderful face. The things of earth will grow greatly dim in the light of His glory and grace. My children have decided to stay before the Lord our mighty King, Jehovah-Jireh.

CHAPTER 9

Activating the Prophetic Gifts

God's original intention was for His people to minister directly to Him as a nation of priests. God longs and invited His people to hear His voice while they serve Him. However, in Deuteronomy 18:15-19, the children of Israel told Moses to speak to us yourself and we will listen. But do not let God speak to us or we will die. In other words, they ask for Moses to be their meditator, changing the plan that God had to communicate with them directly.

Through the New Covenant, Jesus changed all of this back to the Father's original purpose. After the resurrection of Jesus Christ on the day of Pentecost, the Holy Spirit was released to dwell with man. As Christians, we can now all hear His voice and speak His Word (John 20:21-22 Acts 22:17).

CONTINUING GIFTS OF THE SPIRIT

Living a supernatural lifestyle includes operating in all the gifts of the Spirit. In addition, hearing God's voice is enhanced by the revelatory gifts in 1 Corinthians 12:7-11. These gifts include prophecy, words of wisdom, words of knowledge, and the gift of discerning of spirits. As New Testament believers, we all can and should operate in spiritual gifts. However, we need to be biblically taught, trained, and equipped. Our foundation needs to be right. We need to give the Holy Spirit space to practice in a safe environment. Scripture clearly shows us how these gifts operate through agape love and compassion.

1 Corinthians 14:1- 5 (NKJV) says, "Pursue love, and desire spiritual gifts, but especially that you may prophesy. For he who speaks in a tongue does not speak to men but to God, for no one understands him; however, in the spirit he speaks mysteries. But he who prophesies speaks edification and exhortation and comfort to men. He who speaks in a tongue edifies himself, but he who prophesies edifies the church. I wish you all spoke with tongues, but even more that you prophesied; [a]for he who prophesies is greater than he who speaks with tongues, unless indeed he interprets, that the church may receive edification."

My church's (Build Them On The Rock Ministries) vision is to train and equip pastors, ministers, and leaders. Churches and ministries need to operate in these gifts according to the Scripture. As we minister, we want to assure believers that they hear their Father's voice. John 10:27 says that my sheep hears my voice.

The ministry God has called us to shows the body of Christ how to bridge the gap. Based on biblical perspective and principles, we desire for people to function in the authority God has already given us to demonstrate His kingdom on earth.

Activating the gift of prophecy will help you do the following:

1. Prophesy
2. Discerning different spiritual senses
3. Separating God's voice from others voices

When it comes to hearing God, we need to operate in prophetic protocol according to the word to be effective.

Prophecy can sound like a confusing and mystical thing, but it's biblical. It is for today, but how does it all work? I discovered the God of Prophecy.

What is prophecy? Prophecy is supernatural. Prophets by the spirit of God hear His voice then deliver the message. I believe that you cannot prophesy without the function of the spirit. If you are prophesying without God, then you are not prophesying from the correct source. The difference between psychics and prophets. In the kingdom of God, prophets get their information directly from the Holy Spirit. Biblical prophecy is speaking the Words of God by the function of the Holy Spirit.

Who can prophesy? 1 Corinthians 12 lists spiritual gifts that are available to us. When we have the Holy Spirit, everybody can prophesy. However, not all people will choose to prophesy because it's the Holy Spirit that gives us revelation in the first place. All believers can do it. Even if a simple picture coming directly from God can be a profile moment in someone's life. The Holy Spirit gives grace as he wills. 1 Corinthians 12:11 says you get a measure of grace upon your life to operate in that gift. So for some people, it can come really naturally and other people have to work at it.

So what the difference between someone who can prophesy and someone who is a prophet?

We can all operate in the gift of prophecy. However, if someone is called as a prophet, they function differently. We cannot create the gift of healing, wisdom, and discernment. In Ephesians 4, the prophet's function is more of a life calling that is god-given. It's part of who they are and they can't escape it. Prophets who are walking in the fullness of their call have angelic encounters, visions, and dreams. The supernatural flows through their life. I receive mostly visions. A woman on our team has more dreams. Not everyone who prophesises is a prophet. Prophets should be positioned in the local church and operate as a part of a family. I don't believe they should be functioning outside of the local church. It is really good to be commissioned into your call by leadership who recognizes the call and anointing in your life. The other thing to consider is the prophet's realm of influence. Is it a local church level, citywide, or globally? Prophets like Cindy Jacobs, Sharon Stone, Rick Joyner, and Bobby Corner all have a global influence.

How can a Christian learn to prophesy? The Holy Spirit gives a gift that you've received by faith and will teach you how to use it. The Holy Spirit started giving me pictures or Scripture for the people around me. You got to start with those that are around you. You don't go from zero to prophesying over the nation in five minutes. The Scripture says to prophesy according to the proportion of your faith. So when you start off, your faith may be too small to prophesy and overtime will grow. You trust the Holy Spirit to speak to you and build up your trust confidence that you hear correctly. Then read some books, go to a prophetic training course, get activated, and have someone lay hands on you to impart the gift of faith to prophesy. That would be the starting point on how someone should respond to a personal prophecy. When prophecy is being exchanged, two people are involved: the person that is delivering the prophetic word and the person receiving the prophetic word. You have the choice to accept or reject the word. Just because someone has delivered a word to you doesn't mean you have to accept it. The Scripture says, "Judge it." Eat what's good and spit out the bones (1 Thessalonians 5:21). In other words, there may be a mixture of God and the person's flesh. It's up to us now to learn how to judge a prophetic word. It is an invitation for a conversation.

I like to listen to the word repeatedly if it is recorded. I write it out, read it, and pray over it. I ask the Holy Spirit questions. "What is one hundred percent you? What is fluff? What do I need to filter out? We have to make sure no one is trying to take advantage of us. We might have to filter out the fluff or the extra words the person may have added.

I also ask the Lord, "What is for now? What's for later? What's for 14 years down the road?" Discerning God's timing is important to know when things will happen or decipher the metaphors' meaning. Ask Holy Spirit to unpack these.

How do you respond to a prophecy over a group or a church? If it's over a church and you're not in leadership, you don't really have to do anything. It's the leadership's responsibility to take that word and discuss it among themselves. Whether they believe that it is the word of the Lord or not, they go through the same process. What parts are great or have spiritual weight? Is this a word for now? Where do we feel God leading us?

It's about praying. "Lord, is this of you?" Does this bear witness? The Holy Spirit is so faithful. He will give you a strong witness if this is definitely God speaking. If it's not, He doesn't want us to live in deception. That's not His will or who He is. So if you ask Him for discernment, He's going to give it to you. He wants us to have understanding, so pray for wisdom and understanding to know what to do with that word.

If a national word comes in, then the prophet of that nation has a responsibility to judge it.

What else is important to know about the prophetic?

We must prophesy from the foundation that God is good. He redemptive purposes for people, churches, and organizations. We are called to prophesy. We may discern things that are not right but if we set judges in place, our prophetic utterances will not outwork the purpose of the seed and God's will and heart. We need to unlock destiny and set the captive free. We must understand the difference between the gift of discernment and the gift of prophecy. Just because you discern something doesn't mean that God gave you that revelation. You must look to the heart of the Father for what He wants to say about the situation. My children desired the prophetic after realizing that they could not run anymore. They began to open their hearts to their gifts, wanted God to fill them with the prophetic and activate their gifts. It all worked out for the good of them through the Lord Jesus Christ.

CHAPTER 10

What is Saving Grace?

Saving grace is generally used to refer to God's grace to lead a person to salvation. It is based on a variety of biblical principles that emphasizes salvation as a free gift of God's grace rather than something that a person earns through good deeds.

Salvation requires Saving Grace. Romans 3:20 (ESV) says, "For by works of the law no human being[a] will be justified in his sight, since through the law comes knowledge of sin." No amount or level of human accomplishment is good enough to obtain salvation. Isaiah 64:6 teachers that all our righteous deeds are like a polluted garment. Romans 3:21-22 (ESV) says, "But now the righteousness of God has been manifested apart from the law, although the Law and the Prophets bear witness to it— the righteousness of God through faith in Jesus Christ for all who believe. For there is no distinction:"

In addition to the sufficiency of words to obtain salvation, God's grace has provided a way for eternal life through salvation in Jesus Christ. How can a person obtain this salvation in Saving grace? Ephesians 2:8 -9 (ESV) says, "For by grace you have been saved through faith. And this is not your own doing; it is the gift of God, not a result of works, so that no one may boast." A person believes in Jesus by faith and receive salvation by grace as a free gift. Romans 6:23 (ESV) says, " For the wages of sin is death, but the free gift of God is eternal life in Christ Jesus our Lord."

What is a person save from? Salvation includes forgiveness of sin that starts the promise of a new life, eternal life with the Lord. God's work is complete covering the past, present, and future. His work of saving grace makes us a new creation. 2 Corinthians 5:17 says, "Therefore, if anyone is in Christ, he is a new creation. The old has passed away; behold, the new has come." Believers are called live definitely as a new creature. Ephesians 4:23-24 says, " and to be renewed in the spirit of your minds, and to put on the new self, created after the likeness of God in true righteousness and holiness."

Saving grace also removes the Christian from future destruction of eternal punishment and separation from God. They are moving towards the promises of eternity with Christ and His people. The Bible describes a new heaven and new earth. Revelations 21:3- 4 (ESV) is a vision that John had. These Scriptures states, "And I heard a loud voice from the throne saying, "Behold, the dwelling place[a] of God is with man. He will dwell with them, and they will be his people,[b] and God himself will be with them as their God.

He will wipe away every tear from their eyes, and death shall be no more, neither shall there be mourning, nor crying, nor pain anymore, for the former things have passed away."

My children learned that God's saving grace saved them from a dying world full of sin, hate, and pain. They found it was no need to run anymore. All they needed to do was repent and turn their life around and follow the Lord Jesus Christ.

About The Author

Pastor Carol Brown is a woman of vision and virtue. She has lived in Albion, Michigan, most of her life. She got saved at the age of 21 when she gave her heart to Jesus Christ over 30 years ago. She has been in church serving the Lord faithfully. Throughout the years, she has operated strongly in the prophetic, deliverance, and intercession. Carol is married to Victor Brown. They have four children and ten grandchildren who they love very much. Carol and her husband are pastors of Build Them on The Rock Ministries.

Index

A

Abundant Grace, 41
accept, 4, 53
accomplishment, 58
accountable, 4
activated, 53
afflicted, 43
afford, 22
afraid, 25, 35, 36, 37, 38
angelic encounters, 52
anointing, 8, 52
approved, 12
arm, 28, 29

armor, 24
authority, 30, 50

B

battlefield, 23
beautiful, 10, 12, 23
believe, 2, 4, 7, 12, 14, 36, 51, 52, 54, 58
believes, 1, 58
Bible, 1, 2, 6, 7, 37, 40, 59
bless, 7, 31
blind, 4, 5
Bobby Corner, 52
bottoms, 24
bows, 10
breakthrough, 36
breastplate, 24, 25
brethren, 15
Build Them on The Rock Ministries, 62

C

candidate, 14
Carol Brown, 61
challenges, 16
chastisement, 43

child, 6, 8, 14, 15, 16, 28, 44
Christians, 2, 48
Christmases, 10
church, 7, 12, 49, 52, 54, 61
Cindy Jacobs, 52
circumstances, 37
comfort, 49
Commission, 10
conduct, 24
confess, 2
congregation, 13
consecration, 11
Contentment, 32
counseling, 16
COVID-19, 11
curse, 7

D

darkness, 8, 13, 41
David, 8, 20, 44
dead, 3, 42
Deborah, 8
deception, 55
defeat, 34
deliver, 51

deliverance, 36, 61
demonstrate, 50
demoralized, 37
depart, 7
desire, 15, 26, 49, 50
destruction, 11, 59
devil, 3, 21, 29
Different kinds of Tongues, 17
Discerning of the Spirits, 17, 18
discernment, 52, 55, 56
disciple, 29
disciples, 17
discouraged, 37
disheartened, 37
dishonors, 7
dismayed, 25, 35, 37, 38
distinction, 58
distraught, 37
distress, 11
donkey, 17
doors, 26
dormant, 15
doubts, 29
dreams, 52
drivers, 20
drugs, 10

dysfunctionality, 16

E

earth, 7, 45, 46, 50, 59
edifies, 49
elevated, 28
encouraging, 36
enemy, 29, 34, 36, 38
enmity, 44
Enrichment, 40
Esther, 8
eternal life, 2, 3, 58, 59
eternal punishment, 59
eternity, 2, 59
everlasting, 2
exert, 20
exhortation, 49

F

faith, 2, 4, 21, 24, 25, 27, 28, 32, 37, 42, 53, 58
Faith, 17, 18
faithfully, 61
faithfulness, 30
family, 8, 15, 16, 23, 52

fears, 28, 29
field, 11
fight, 23, 25, 35, 37, 38
finances, 15, 31
fire, 32
firm, 24, 35, 36, 38
flesh, 16, 21, 22, 40, 41, 53
fluff, 54
focus, 32, 36, 46
forsake, 20, 31
fortified, 22
Fred and Clara McGee, 7
free, 8, 12, 20, 24, 31, 56, 57, 58
freedom, 28, 30
frustration, 16
function, 50, 51, 52
future, 20, 32, 59

G

generation, 7
generational blessing, 7
gentleness, 28
gift, 2, 3, 4, 9, 10, 11, 12, 14, 15, 20, 27, 28, 32, 39, 40, 48, 50, 51, 52, 53, 56, 57, 58

gifts, 10, 12, 13, 14, 15, 16, 17, 23, 26, 28, 48, 49, 51, 56
Gifts of healing, 18
Gifts of Healing, 17
glory, 41, 45, 46
God, 1, 2, 3, 4, 6, 7, 8, 10, 11, 12, 13, 14, 15, 16, 17, 19, 20, 21, 22, 23, 24, 25, 26, 27, 28, 29, 30, 31, 32, 34, 35, 36, 37, 38, 39, 40, 41, 42, 43, 44, 47, 48, 49, 50, 51, 53, 54, 55, 56, 57, 58, 59, 60
godliness, 22
goodness, 29
Gospel, 4
grace, 2, 15, 16, 22, 24, 25, 27, 29, 40, 41, 46, 51, 57, 58, 59, 60
grandparents, 7
Grief Bearer, 43
grows, 7
guilt, 4, 5

H

hearts, 12, 30, 56
heaven, 11, 28, 42, 45, 59
helmet, 24
hibernation, 11
holiness, 59

holy, 24
hopeless, 21
humble, 22
humility, 4
husband, 15, 16, 62

I

identity, 11, 12
ignorant, 15
image, 12, 26
imagery, 24
impenetrable, 21
imperishable, 42
influence, 52
intercession, 61
Interpretation, 18
Interpretation of Tongues, 18
interprets, 49
intimate, 26
Israelites, 36

J

Jacob, 8
Jehoshaphat, 25, 35, 36

Jehovah-Jireh, 46
Jerusalem, 17, 25, 35, 38
Jesus, 2, 3, 4, 5, 16, 17, 20, 24, 25, 28, 32, 40, 41, 42, 43, 44, 45, 46, 48, 56, 58, 60, 61
Jesus Christ, 2, 24, 28, 40, 42, 45, 48, 56, 58, 60, 61
Judgment, 5

K

King, 25, 35, 36, 42, 44, 45, 46
Kingdom of God, 7
knowledge, 15, 48, 58

L

leaders, 49
leadership, 52, 54
lesson, 25
level, 11, 52, 58
life, 2, 8, 12, 13, 16, 19, 21, 23, 24, 29, 31, 40, 41, 51, 52, 58, 59, 60, 61
light, 8, 13, 40, 41, 46
lusts, 24
lyrics, 10

M

manifest, 17
marriage, 15
meditator, 48
merchant, 11
message, 4, 17, 51
metaphors, 54
ministry, 2, 6, 50
miraculous, 4
miscommunication, 15
mixture, 53
money, 10, 31
morning, 29, 30
Moses, 47, 48
mother, 6, 7
mourning, 60
mouth, 2
multitude, 25
mysteries, 49

N

nations, 6
need, 3, 4, 19, 21, 26, 30, 31, 35, 37, 38, 40, 42, 48, 49, 50, 54, 55, 60

new creation, 59
nightclub, 10

O

obedience, 22
operate, 16, 19, 48, 49, 50, 51, 52
oppresses, 30
organization, 8
organizations, 55
overcome, 16, 36, 38, 41
overnight, 8

P

pagan, 35
pain, 29, 60
pandemic, 11
paper, 10, 26
party, 3
pastors, 49, 62
peace, 21, 24, 43, 44, 46
pearls, 11
perish, 1
Pharisees, 4, 5
plan, 20, 40, 48

position, 25, 35, 36, 38
powerful, 28, 36, 37
powerful army, 36
prayer, 7, 26, 36, 38
prayer meeting, 7
presence, 20
priests, 47
process, 54
promise, 21, 22, 59
promises, 22, 28, 36, 59
Prophecy, 17, 18, 50
prophesied, 36, 49
prophesy, 49, 51, 52, 53, 55
Prophesy, 50
prophet, 6, 51, 52, 55
prophetic, 50, 53, 54, 55, 56, 61
prophetic training, 53

Q

quarantine, 11

R

reconciled, 2
reconciliation, 2

relationship, 10, 26, 32
religious institutions, 4
religious system, 27
repent, 60
resistance, 21
responsibility, 54, 55
resurrection, 25, 41, 42, 48
revealed, 16, 26, 42
revelation, 11, 12, 18, 24, 51, 56
revelatory gifts, 48
Rick Joyner, 52
Righteousness Judge, 45
Risen Savior, 41
robe of righteousness, 12

S

Sabbath, 4
salvation, 3, 4, 10, 12, 21, 24, 25, 35, 36, 38, 57, 58
Samaritan woman, 16
Satan, 15, 21, 22
saved, 1, 2, 3, 58, 60, 61
Sharon Stone, 52
sheep, 43, 49
shelters, 8

shoulder, 38, 44
sin, 3, 41, 58, 59, 60
sins, 43
slain, 45
Son, 1, 2, 40, 41, 43, 45
sorrow, 43
spiritual gifts, 15, 48
spiritual weight, 55
spiritually, 10
storm, 12
stresses, 10
struggles, 10
Styrofoam, 4
submission, 21
successful, 21
Sufficient, 40
summit, 21
supernatural, 48, 50, 52
Supernatural, 17
Surrendering, 28, 29, 32

T

throne, 44, 45, 59
time, 8, 10, 12, 15, 20, 21, 32, 34, 36, 40, 42, 44
tongue, 49

tragedy, 11
trained, 6, 48
transformation, 8, 27
treasures, 12, 26
triumphant ruler, 44
trouble, 33
trust, 28, 30, 32, 53
truth, 4, 12, 23, 24, 41

U

unhappiness, 11
universe, 30
unquenchable, 40
unwrap, 9, 10, 12, 13, 20, 23

V

value, 11, 27, 28
Victory, 25
virtue, 61
virus, 11
visions, 52
voice, 47, 48, 49, 50, 59
vulnerable, 30

W

wages, 3, 58
wisdom, 45, 48, 52, 55
witness, 55, 58
womb, 6
Wonderful Counselor, 44
Word of Knowledge, 15, 16, 17
Word of Wisdom, 15, 17, 18
Wordy ruler, 45
Working of Miracles, 17
works, 2, 3, 58
world, 1, 2, 5, 10, 27, 40, 41, 46, 60
worries, 28
worshipping, 35

Y

youth department, 7

www.ingramcontent.com/pod-product-compliance
Lightning Source LLC
Chambersburg PA
CBHW052118110526
44592CB00013B/1656